36 HOURS AT THE INTERSECTION OF

MERCY

AND

GRACE

✳ ✳ ✳

LURA'S STORY

Fredna DeCarlo

ISBN 978-1-64300-131-9 (Paperback)
ISBN 978-1-64300-132-6 (Digital)

Covenant Books, Inc.
11661 Hwy 707
Murrells Inlet, SC 29576
www.covenantbooks.com

PREFACE

*L*et me be clear from the beginning—this is not a story about groundbreaking medical interventions, although this story includes some very incredible medical personnel ranging from medical secretaries to physicians, EMTs, paramedics, fireman, and nurses. But instead, it is a story of spiritual mediation and intercession.

This is a story of a beautiful awaking of spiritual grace—one which tells how the suffering of one little girl brought grace and hope to so many people, and one that will also look closely at the long hours of heartbreak and fear for those who love her. It will also look at how those thirty-six hours seemed like an eternity to us.

This experience drew together so many unlikely people. These people not only became friends, but some of them will be friends for life. These thirty-six hours touched and brought together strangers, friends, loved ones, believers and non- believers alike.

I found a quote by Tony Evans that sums up the story within entirely: "*Sometimes, God allows something to happen in your life that only God can fix, so that you'll get to see him fix it.*"

Let me also be very clear on one thing: spirituality was never my strong suit. Early on in my life my path began a twisting, winding, bumpy, country, city, back-alley kind of way. I could go into great details about this, but it really has nothing to do with this story.

It was said only to establish the fact that I was not a believer in miracles, much less did I have a close relationship with God although I was working my way back into the fold as best I could. I have been going to Lakewood for several years; but as we all know, change takes time—or a miracle.

I used to laugh and say some people see the light because they are looking for it, and others because they feel the heat. I believe at that time I was somewhere in the middle of that statement.

I had always left the spirituality business up to my brother, his wife, or my sister for many years. The second reason I won't go into great detail is because God says when you ask for forgiveness your sins are cast into the sea of forgetfulness, and that is where I will leave them.

During these long, hard thirty-six hours, I was on the inside of this circle of faith. As I look back, though, I can see it so clearly as if I was standing on the outside looking in through a window.

The helplessness of fear and doubt tried to overtake our family and friends during these hours. But the light of faith outshined the oppression in the darkest hours of our trial.

My brother and sister-in-law and their brothers and sisters in Christ were able to share the warmth and the light of faith with others who were caught in their own darkness, fear, doubt, and battle inside the ICU.

I watched as people who would only glance in a passerby's direction—a quick peek as they passed. They would glance up as you passed the glass doors of their child's ICU bed. Desperation and fear etched in their hearts and on their faces.

In those brief seconds of eye contact, stories were told—stories that would take a lifetime to speak out loud. Then they would close their circle again, sitting and waiting beside their child's ICU bed.

Then slowly, one by one they began to watch and look for my brother and his brother in Christ. As soon as they saw them pass by their rooms, they would quickly get up and come out into the hall to ask if they could step inside their circle and pray for their child.

So many times even in my brother's own terror, he found the strength to pray for someone else. He said when he walked into one room, a small boy probably not even three was lying there on a ventilator with his chest wide open. He could see this child's beating heart as he prayed. The weight and magnitude of his prayers truly humbled him.

I also heard him say on more than one occasion, "Inside this ICU, there is no such thing as race, class, believer, or nonbeliever. This is a wing in the hospital where loved ones wait for the unthinkable to happen."

Then they'd breathe deeply in relief as each hour passed, leaving their children still holding on to life.

Everyone inside the ICU are like soldiers whether they want to be or not. You form a deep bond—raw, honest, and quick. You know each other's horror and can truly relate as another parent waits for the unimaginable and inconceivable.

*****

On July 31, Belinda Fleming—a longtime friend and neighbor of my parents—posted a picture on Facebook. A dove had flown into her glass door. The oil on the dove's feathers left a complete and perfect outline of it on the glass. You could even see the beak in the middle of the head.

Belinda took a picture of the glass door from inside her house. The door faces out toward my parent's home. A strange phenomenon occurred.

The image appeared as an angel standing in my mother's front yard. Of course, when you are told what the image is you can see it clearly for what it is. But my eyes insisted that it was an angel.

I was startled and taken aback. I could not take my eyes off of the image. For several minutes I was completely transfixed. Then when I really thought about it I became frightened. I thought something must have happened to one of my parents.

I immediately called my mom. I quickly told her about Belinda's picture. I explained to her what it was, but to my eyes it was a picture of an angel standing in our yard. I asked her if my father was okay. She said as far as she knew he was fine, and that she was fine as well.

She was at work. She was on her rural mail route that she has driven for years. She is now seventy-eight, and she is still at it. She drives the loop from Menard to London and back to Menard.

So I told her I would call her back later. I found I could not leave the picture alone. I kept going back to it and looking at it. I would leave and go do something around the house, but before I knew it I was back looking at the picture. My mind still insisted it was an angel in my mom's front yard.

Something about that picture tugged at the back of my mind. It was like fiddling with a knot. It kept wrestling its way back to the forefront of my mind. It did not matter how many times I pushed it back. It would rise to the front over and over again.

My sister Torrie in San Antonio had seen the image as well. She had gone to work, but the first chance she got she had called our mother too. Her story was pretty much the same as mine. There was a large white angel standing in their front yard.

Several other people on Facebook who knew our parents called as well. My mother told them she was fine, and as soon as she got home she would check on my father. He is ill. He has been in renal failure and on dialysis for several years, and at the time he was not doing very well.

So of course my mother's curiosity was peaked. She wanted to see the picture we were all talking about. The problem is that she does not even know how to turn a computer on, much less have a Facebook account. She was also out in the country, driving. She would have to wait. She could have waited until she got home and have my daddy pull it up for her, but as we all know curiosity makes us inpatient.

When I called her back, I told mom my first thought was that it was an angel. Maybe it was warning us something happened to or was going to happen to my father. These were my sister's same thoughts. Others said the same thing crossed their minds as well. They also were concerned and wondered if mom was okay. That is why they called.

Mom really had no way to conceive what we were talking about. You can try and imagine what someone is trying to describe to you, but the truth is even the most skilled artist's vision is skewed by personal experience.

So when she got back to the post office thirty minutes later, she asked Gennie (who also happens to be Belinda's daughter-in-law) and a woman that works at the post office with her to pull up Facebook on her phone.

She told them about everyone calling to tell her there was an angel standing in her yard, so she really wanted to see it. She asked Gennie if she could please show her what we were talking about.

She said when she saw the angel, she got chills all over her body. Instantly, she knew exactly why we were all talking about it and why we were so moved by it. She felt like it was a warning or an omen as well. She wanted to get home as quick as possible and check on daddy.

She had already talked to me and my sister, so she knew we were fine. My brother Lanier (Duder) does not have a Facebook account either, so she knew that was why he hadn't called. She called him to talk to him, tell him the story and to make sure that he and his family was all right too.

Little did we know two days later our lives would be changed in a profound and unexpected way that from that moment on, we would look at the world and life with different eyes and hearts.

Hours 1–5

August 2, 2016 was like any other Tuesday in the West Texas town of San Angelo. It was hot and dry, and when I say hot I mean sweltering. The temperature hovered around one hundred degrees in the shade. There wasn't a cloud in the sky to break the sunlight from beating down on you.

Lura was at Michael's with her mother, shopping for craft supplies. This was where the normal every other Tuesday went down the drain.

Lura, my niece, was looking at something on a shelf above eye level. She reached up to pick it up. As she did, she called out to her mother saying, "Hey, look at this."

Suddenly right before Lora Lea's eyes, Lura collapsed on the floor. She was having a seizure. This seizure forever changed her life and the lives of those who love her. I know these words sound rather dramatic for someone "just having a seizure."

I have been a registered nurse for almost thirty years. So when I say I know people have had seizures multiple times a day every day—and a whole slew of them are children—I mean I not only know, but I understand as well.

People will say, "What's so devastating about that? You have a seizure; it lasts for a few seconds or maybe even a few minutes, then your brain will rest in what is called a postical state. After that, your life goes on."

Only, that wasn't what happened in Lura's case. This is the reason I was compelled to write Lura's story of grace, mercy, and favor.

In a world that has grown numb to tragedy and devastation, we are oblivious to it. We walk past or see through people in crisis every day. There is never a day that goes by that there isn't some form of devastation taking place. It is happening either to someone we know or even strangers, except they become a part of our world with 24–7 news.

Lura's illness was sandpaper to my blurred vision or blindness. If I am honest with myself to the calluses on my heart. When you are a witness to the things that go on in our world, you become almost desensitized to others' sufferings—not because you are cruel or uncaring but because the human heart and mind can only take so much. Since Lura's horrible experience, I spend a lot more time every day looking and listening for miracles. I look for and watch God move in our world—his subtle hand at work, or his wrath. Either way, there is beauty and grace.

What I have found is that miracles actually are everywhere. They are happening all the time. We have just become blind to their presence. It is like we have scabs on our emotions. It dulls our ability to see past the ready given answer and keeps us from looking for something greater than those simple answers.

Our world is a world where technology engulfs the mind of us all. We have been trained to believe there is a quick and easy fix for everything: a gadget, a pill, or even a standard phrase of apology. We walk through our lives almost on rote memory. Our lives have become like the internet. Answers and cures are seconds away and at our fingertips 24–7.

We have become people of words. It is so easy to get dressed up on Sunday and go to church. It is easy to sing and praise God. It is very simple once or twice a week for an hour to say we believe the promises in the Bible. It is simple to quote back scriptures from rote memory or from a place in our heart that still thinks it believes and understands the power of God.

It is a totally different ball game to actually put that trust to the test. When there is absolutely nothing else you can do but stand on those promises, to understand the gravity of putting your toes to the plumb line and drawing in a slow, deep breath. Then taking that one giant step over it; offering your child up into the hands of God, believing he will protect and heal her; then hand her back to your waiting arms.

I am, in no uncertain terms, implying that our experience of grace reflects on someone else's experience, or that the belief or journey of others who have lost loved ones to horrible tragedies or illness is a result of less faith or belief. I do not believe that nor do I understand why some live and others have to die; that understanding and knowledge belongs to God.

*****

As I said earlier, I have been a nurse for almost thirty years. I have witnessed unbelievable miracles of healing and promise. Like I said before, we have become numb. At the time when it was oblivious God had intervened on someone's behalf, it is chalked up to good medical practice or an unknown reason. Before anyone gets riled up. I am not saying it is always God or only God. In those twenty-seven years, I have seen some truly amazing things happen because of incredible nurses and doctors.

On the other side of the coin, I had also witnessed the completely engulfing horrors of loss and death. When we as health-care providers go home, and in the stillness of the night, we question ourselves if there was anything else we could have done, or did we miss some small sign? Even when you know the answer is no, you still lie awake at night.

You will lie awake crying for the family that has lost their loved one. The old and young alike, it does not make the suffering of their loved ones any less.

*****

I want you to understand on a core level that Lura's parents had already buried one child. Lura's older brother, Little Rodney, died at birth. So please, do not for one second believe or think that they had never experienced the soul-ripping grief of losing a child, because that grief has lived inside their hearts, minds, and souls for almost two decades now.

I know they have faith and believe that he is with God. I also know that it does not for one second take away their pain. I see it in their eyes behind every smile.

So what I will try to do in this story is share with you our thirty-six hours of grace and mercy. I will try my best to make you see even in our hours of greatest belief. We found ourselves fighting hand-to-hand combat in our hearts and minds against the enemy, which goes by the names of fear and doubt. These two emotions tried to weasel their way in, constantly seeking and searching for a crack in our wall of faith and trust. I found that doubt, when it manifests, can be as flexible and elusive as smoke. This elusiveness allows it to penetrate even the slightest crack. Sometimes, that fissure is so small that your heart's eyes can't see it or even know it is there when you search your heart. But once it gets inside, fear and doubt can work unbelievable destruction. It will try to chip away your faith like a jackhammer.

With all of that said, let's go back to the beginning and start at the very second this story actually started—August 2, 2016, at three o'clock in the afternoon, the instant Lura collapsed, having a seizure.

My sister-in-law is a teacher and had on more than one occasion helped a student or two who was having a seizure. So she knew what was happening the second she saw Lura going down. She also knew what to do.

I am quite sure the teacher in her kicked in automatically; but underneath—I believe—the complete panic of a mother was screaming as she rushed to Lura's side. She called out for someone to call 911.

I remembered hearing her say, "I knew what was happening the minute I saw her, but I couldn't get to her in time to keep her from hitting the floor."

This was the first miracle. Most people would think nothing of it nor give it a second thought. But for someone to fall without the ability to break their fall and for their head to bounce off the cement floor, her head bounced off the floor and then hit it again and settled there. There was no subdural hematoma or other contusions, but who knew that fact then, because she was unresponsive and seizing.

I know this was horrifying for her mother because not only was it something new but also she was helpless to help her. Lura never had a seizure before. As a matter of fact, other than severe reflux when she was a baby, she had hardly ever been sick.

Lora Lea (Lura's mom) made sure Lura wasn't biting her tongue or her cheek, and her airway was open. She supported her neck and rolled her over on her side. Then she took out her cell phone and called Duder (Lura's dad). She was screaming for him to come fast because Lura was seizing. Then she sat and watched as her child had one seizure after another while she waited for the ambulance and for Duder to arrive.

*****

My brother's world belongs to this child. I can't begin to understand the fear and confusion that must have struck him like a baseball bat to the face. He told me that he and two of his employees had gone to town to get an ice cream cone. It was so hot that day. He thought they could all benefit from the coolness.

Actually, this was the second time God had intervened. With him being in town, he was about fifteen minutes closer to Lura and Lora Lea than if he had been out at Wall at work.

Instantly, he turned and drove as fast as he could to Michael's. His mind and body were headed to his wife and daughter. His heart was crying out to God to intervene.

15

I really believe that both of Lura's parents thought this was going to be a one-and-done thing. Like all of us when something out of the blue happens to us or someone we love, we have a tendency to rationalize things. We try to explain them to our terrified minds. We tell ourselves this is a freak event.

So the terror ramped up for my brother when he arrived at Michael's. Lora Lea and Lura were together; and Lura was still on the floor, seizing. He had also beaten the EMS in arriving there. He told me later that he had been so terrified that all he could do was drive and pray that God would protect his daughter. He kept asking himself and God, "How did we get here?"

Lura was still having seizures and continued to seize even after the EMS and firemen paramedics arrived. They began the task of taking a quick history. It is very important to know if there had ever been seizures before and if the patient had had seizures in the past is this seizure different than the previous ones.

They stabilized her neck, started an IV, and began administering anti-seizure medications. The standard algorithm for pediatric seizures that were not caused by fever or a witnessed head injury was to first check their blood glucose level. Believe it or not, correcting a blood glucose level in a pediatric patient is more important than stopping the seizure. A lot of times, a seizure is a symptom of an abnormal blood glucose. The abnormal blood glucose is also a sign of trouble on the way for a nondiabetic pediatric patient.

Her blood glucose level was within normal limits, so they administered dextrose and midazolam or diazepam IV (if you already have an IV going; if you don't, you can squirt it inside their nose. It has a rapid absorption time as well).

*****

Status epilepticus is a condition that is medically described as having two or more seizures in succession without a period of consciousness or recovery in between. This is a true emergency and requires rapid airway management and transport to the hospital. At the time of EMS's arrival, Lura had over ten seizures without recovery or consciousness.

The arrival of EMS allowed Duder and Lora Lea permission to go from trying to medically take care of their child to being terrified and lost parents. Unfortunately, this also allowed the truth of their helplessness to settle in. All they could do was watch the EMS work on their "world" lying on Michael's floor.

When the EMS saw that after two doses of anti-seizure medicine the seizures continued and there was no pause between them, they advanced to the next step. They loaded her in the ambulance. Lora Lea went with her in the ambulance. Duder followed behind in his pickup.

All the way from Michael's to the hospital, her seizures continued despite medical intervention. She continued to have seizures, and they continued to give her multiple medications to stop her seizures. When the seizures continued after the maximum dosage allowed outside the hospital was given, they gave her a dose of Narcan. This is a medicine used to treat drug overdoses.

They were grasping at straws at this point and hoped anything would work. Lura's condition was critical.

The sad truth is in this day and age you never know about drug use. Even the ones you would never expect can fool you. It was a "just-in-case" move. Being a nurse, I understood this thought process completely.

She could have, somehow, either gotten into a drug accidently or on purpose. The Narcan did nothing. So, that avenue was ruled out. All they knew was she was having continuous seizures, and nothing was stopping them. So, of course, she remained unresponsive. Duder said that he asked God again, "How did we get here? And please, protect my child."

I know my brother and sister-in-law, and my heart lurches into my throat every time I think of those moments. The fear and helplessness they must have felt breaks my heart for them.

They arrived at the emergency room. The EMTs and paramedics rolled Lura into a trauma room. Then what appears to the outside world, a needless repeating of words and actions occurred.

*****

As nurses and doctors, we think and act as we listen. Quickly, the nurses and doctor did their initial assessment, unhooked her from the ambulance's monitors and hooked her up on their monitors.

The IV was transferred to their equipment. The doctor started ordering tests, and nurses and ancillary departments began to complete these tests. They administered more medications to stop her seizures with absolutely no results. Duder and Lora Lea could do nothing but stand and watch and answer questions as best they could.

The truth was they had no idea what was happening either. While their mouths and minds were answering questions, their hearts were praying.

A few minutes later, which must have seemed like seconds and at the same time hours, the transport orderly showed up to take Lura to radiology for a CT scan of her brain. Her parents could not go in with her, so they were left standing at the door.

This was when they started calling family, friends, and brothers and sisters in Christ and cried out to them to start praying for Lura as well as the nurses and doctors caring for her. They had no information to give except that for no apparent reason Lura started having seizures and was still having them continuously. She not regained consciousness since this started at 3 p.m.

Of course, their first calls were to their parents—Lura's grandparents. Then, calls started going out to other family members and to brothers and sisters in Christ. This had set off a ripple that within less than thirty minutes had reached six of the seven continents.

I know that so many people will say there is nothing special about having that deep of a ripple because of the internet these days.

I just ask that you consider the gravity of the amount of people praying for one little girl.

One set of her grandparents live in Menard, a little town sixty-five miles away. They immediately started loading up. They have raised their great-granddaughter Ireland since birth. So they had to make arrangements for her. There was no sense taking a five-year-old to the emergency room's waiting room where emotions were running high. They also had no idea how long they would be there.

They called a family friend and the woman who had taken care of Ireland since she was little—Carolina Ortega. Of course, Carolina said, "Bring her here and don't think about it again. If she is still here at bedtime, let her stay the night." Five minutes later, they dropped her off and were on their way.

I am sure that sixty-five miles felt like a million miles away. On their way to San Angelo, they called my sister Torrie and I. We are Lura's aunts. Duder is our brother.

All they knew was Lura collapsed suddenly and was having seizures. She was in the emergency room in San Angelo, unresponsive. They would tell us more when they knew something.

Then my mother called Becky Callan, a friend of Lora Lea's that lives in San Angelo. She immediately came to the emergency room and stayed with them until Lura was loaded in the ambulance to head to Mathis Field.

*****

Torrie lives in San Antonio and goes to Cornerstone Church. She made calls to the prayer line immediately. They started to pray for Lura.

I received the call from my mom. While we were talking, I told my family what was going on. I placed my own call to my church, Lakewood's prayer warrior line. They immediately prayed for Lura. The prayers for Lura were now spreading the networks of prayer warriors, friends, and families.

I have to admit my first reaction was confusion and fear. Lura had always been such a healthy, vibrant child. My second reaction was the same as the EMTs—did she get into anything accidently?

I knew it would not be an on-purpose thing. At thirteen, she still took liquid Tylenol. She could not swallow a pill no matter how she tried. That still did not rule out the possibility of someone slipping something in her drink or her coming into contact with something that had been placed on one of the shelves. Really, she could have come into contact with something deadly in a thousand different places.

The truth is we live in a world today where acts of terror are always in the front of everyone's minds. This is a sad fact and one that people will try to say, "Maybe that would be a possibility in Houston but not San Angelo." The problem is that is no longer a true statement either.

Time seemed to be flying by on my side. I kept thinking, *It is already 3:30 p.m. Why haven't we heard anything yet?* Of course, that was the aunt in me. The nurse in me knew that lab tests, CT scans, and other procedures took time. I also knew for my brother and sister-in-law these minutes were passing by in the slow motion of clarity and fast-forward blurs at the same time. As of 4 p.m., she was still having seizures and still had not regained consciousness.

In the meantime, all the lab reports started coming back normal. The lactic acid was normal. The CBC, BNP, BMP, and drug screen came back normal and negative for drugs or alcohol. The CT scan came back normal as well. This should have been good news. This meant there had not been a stroke or an unwitnessed head injury, at some point, her parent's didn't know about. Thankfully, there wasn't a brain tumor secretly and silently growing unnoticed either.

The problem was Lura had not regained consciousness yet. She would seize and then go postictal (which was the period that immediately followed a seizure until the person regained consciousness) except Lura wasn't regaining consciousness. Instead, she would have another seizure. Please also know that during this time period she continued to receive anti-seizure medication.

The phone calls that had gone out while Lura was in CT scan were starting to spread in the regions of the world as well. Prayer warriors were calling prayer warriors, and brothers were calling brothers in Emmaus. Within a very short time, teachers, students, bus drivers, lawyers, doctors, nurses, friends, and families near and as far away as South Africa were praying not only for Lura but for her parents as well.

Their friend and brother in Christ, Chad Leutwyler, was in a little West Texas town called Robert Lee, about thirty-one miles away. When he got the news, he began to pray. He told me later that when he heard Duder's voice, he felt the sense of urgency and fear in his voice.

After Duder told him what was happening, his first response was to pray with Duder over the phone then and there inside the car dealership.

He said he remembers going back inside and telling his salesman, "I need to go, and I need to go now."

I joke and say this is a miracle too. I am being funny but not really. All the paperwork for purchasing his new car was completed in five minutes. He was on the road to San Angelo in less than ten minutes from the time he talked to Duder.

He rushed to the Community Hospital's emergency room in San Angelo. He told me later, "I hate to speed and break the law. I don't like to, but I must admit my foot was a little heavy." He chuckled.

He made that thirty-one-mile trip in less than twenty minutes. On his arrival, he found Lura still unresponsive.

He immediately prayed for her, Duder, and Lora Lea. Then he went outside to call his wife to let her know what was happening. He was then sentenced to the same sentence as the rest of us—he waited.

I did not know Chad before this, but he was a dear friend to my brother. As a matter of fact, he is almost a brother and definitely a brother in Christ. I can say now after spending time with him in the trenches, he is a man of great faith. He loves my brother and his family, and set in to do his part.

He prayed for Lura without ceasing. When the time came, he helped get Duder ready for the trip that lay ahead. The doctor had just told them that Lura was critical. Lura needed to get to a bigger hospital and soon.

She needed a specialist that they just didn't have in San Angelo. He felt if she was going to have a chance to make it, she needed to go and go as soon as possible.

Chad went out and called his wife again. He asked her to bring his oldest son to drive the new car home. Then he asked her to bring him an overnight bag. He said his wife knew the minute he asked for a bag that it was serious.

She arrived with the bag and their son to drive the car home. He said he told her what was going on in greater detail. He then said they prayed as a family for Lura and her parents and for wisdom for the doctors and nurses. Then he headed back inside.

Duder told me that when he looks back at it, God moved Chad into their lives two years ahead of this experience. Chad came to Wall and was preaching at the Veribest Baptist Church. He still needed a job to make ends meet, and he came to work for Duder. During those two years they traveled many miles together, driving the school buses both locally and taking kids to events out of town. They spent many hours talking about life and God and his love.

Chad was there for my family during this time, unwavering. He never left my brother's side till this was over. Then after they got home to San Angelo, he was there with them during those scary first weeks. After that, God moved Chad down the road to a church in the Dallas area. This move took place about two months after Lura's illness.

We all knew God put Chad in our lives to stand with us on the promises of God. He prayed and believed with us. He was able to stand and see God work. There was nothing subtle about it. It was powerful and humbling.

*****

So, the transfer process began. This was also a clear example of God moving people into Lura's life either directly or indirectly. The unit secretary who was to start initiating the transfer activity had come into Lura's life indirectly.

Earlier that summer, Lora Lea had done a walk to Emmaus. One of the pilgrims on this walk was the unit secretary. She later told Duder and Lora Lea that she worked her behind/off, getting the best of the best that she could arrange for them.

Another incident was one of the nurses in the emergency room that afternoon was the mother of the child that Lora Lea had assisted with seizures at school. There was already mutual friendship and respect. This created a personal attachment for the both of them.

When transfers from one hospital to another take place, on the hospital side of it there is organized chaos. We were aware that it looks like nothing is being done to people stressed out and impatient. To them, it seems like we are idling. Anyone who has ever been through this process knows this process does not happen as quickly as one wants.

At this point, the family and loved ones of the patient feel each minute as days. They'd glance at the clock and knew that hours have passed, only to find the clock has moved maybe ten minutes.

On the other side of that story, nurses have begun to complete orders, make copies of the chart that needed to go with the patient. The doctor starts calling the receiving hospital because there has to be a receiving doctor. Then nurses have to start the process of transferring the patient since San Antonio was a little over 235 miles away from San Angelo. The fact that Lura was very critical, she would have to go by air.

This was where God started putting the best of the best in Lura's path again, unknown to any of us at that time. I believe this was the beginning of the answering of prayers.

The life-flight helicopter from San Antonio Methodist Children's Hospital was contacted. Soon the team leader returned the call. They had news no one wanted to hear. The flight team had been in the air too long, and another team had been contacted. This team was in the process of coming in.

Thirty minutes later when they called back, we were told they were going to have to send a fixed wing instead of a helicopter. Then the other boot fell. It would take a while longer to get going.

The problem with this was at this point, Lura had already been in the emergency room over two hours. She was becoming more unstable with each passing minute. Her parents were told she was becoming urgently critical.

This new news forced her parents, family, friends, and church members to do the hardest thing in life. Once again, they were forced to wait.

Again, this was God putting the best of the best in Lura's path. One of the other nurses in the emergency room later told Duder and Lora Lea that they had worked with the flight nurse that came with the fixed wing before. She was one of the best flight nurses she had ever worked with.

Later on, we would learn that as this nurse was walking toward the emergency room in San Antonio to get in the ambulance that would take them to the airport. She grabbed her friend and flight respiratory therapist to fly along. She said, "Hey, I am going to San Angelo. Come go with me."

Later in this story, you will see how this little unsuspecting action was also an act of God. He kept lining people up in Lura's path.

One of the hardest lessons I have learned in life is to believe what I say I believe. It is easy to say I trust God to protect my loved ones when everything is good or even when things are a little rocky. But to stand on my faith when I am looking death in the face is not always the same thing, that is, when the opposing forces in life taunt me with doubt. That kind of doubt. This doubt is usually brought on by fear.

At first, you don't even realize that it has snuck in, not until you noticed it has been in the background, ratcheting up your fear every time you looked at one of the nurses in the eyes and see that look that says, "We have got to get this kid out of here. She needs to be where there is a specialist." Or when you see the doctor making repeated calls to the receiving hospital, clearly wondering where the helicopter, fixed wing, or whatever it is.

I have been in both sides of this nightmare. I still am not sure which side is worse. I was certain as these minutes stretched on for Duder and Lora Lea that every second, they felt the weight of these seconds as millenniums.

I also promise you: there is nothing more horrifying for nurses than to have someone's child's life in their hands, and everything they do is just not working.

My mom called me back and told me they were still waiting. She also said that Lura was still unresponsive, and they were waiting on a fixed wing air ambulance. At that point I told my mother, "I am going. I am leaving right now. I have to throw a few clothes in a bag for me and Imili (my twelve-year-old daughter) then I would be on my way on my way."

What I hadn't told my mother was that I had flushed all our bills that morning. I had also just come home from the store where I bought two weeks' worth of groceries. I had exactly twenty-four dollars to my name. Luckily, I had filled up my car while I was out doing errands. That action ensured I had a full tank of gas to get there.

I remembered calling my youngest son, Sterling, as I loaded up my car. I asked him if he had any cash on him. He laughed and said, "About twenty bucks, why?"

I was in the act of asking if I could borrow it when my middle son, Demi, and his wife, Marce, and the kids drove up. He knew immediately something was wrong. He later told me his first thought was that something was wrong with my father once again because he had been sick for a couple of years. He asked. "What's wrong?"

I told him about Lura. I told him she was still unresponsive and waiting on a fixed wing air ambulance to get her to San Antonio. He was listening to me and talking to my younger son at the same time I was talking to him. I remember saying to my youngest son, "I will be all right. If I can just get there, I will be okay. Imili and I can stay in the waiting room around the clock. I will find a way to feed her. I will be fine as long as there is coffee in the waiting room."

I threw my suitcase in the back seat of the Tahoe. I told my son I would be there in a few minutes to pick up the twenty dollars. That now made it forty-four dollars. I knew I could feed Imili for a few days on that. At this point, we had no idea what we were looking at time wise.

As I said earlier, I also have a sister that lives in San Antonio. I knew she would make sure Imili ate. Then Demi, my middle son, took out his wallet and handed me one of his credit cards. He said, "Just use it."

I was so touched. The problem was I didn't have any time left to convey how touched I was. I just hugged him and his wife and whispered a thank-you. I look back and see God was making a way for me to go. It was divine timing. If they had come five minutes later, I would have already been on the road. Once again, God had stepped in. I pulled out of my driveway and called my mom back to let her know I was rolling.

She told me Lura was still unresponsive when I talked to her. She said they were still waiting for the air ambulance. Mom said the lobby at Community Hospital was full of people praying for Lura and sending out texts and e-mails to have others pray as well.

While I was sitting at the stop sign, I had Imili log on to my Facebook page on my phone. Prayers were being said in almost every country in the world. We have friends that are like family in Europe. I have family in Australia. I have in-laws in Asia, both the Philippines and Korea. I have a true-and-dear friend who lives in South Africa. We also have friends and family in Mexico and South America. So when I say the world was praying for Lura, I mean the *world*.

I took the back roads between Missouri City, and Katy trying to cut time off my drive. There is a sort of, kind of shortcut if you know what roads to take. On any given trip, for me, it takes over three-and-a-half hours to get from my house to San Antonio. I was determined to be there as soon as possible and hopefully not long after Lura arrived. I also knew I had to be safe. I certainly didn't need a ticket. I knew as well getting in a wreck and being injured or killed ourselves would help no one. My thoughts echoed Chad's. My foot was a little heavy.

I had Imili call my mother for me when we got to Katy. As I merged up on I-10 West, the news was still the same—Lura was still unresponsive, still having seizures, and still waiting for the air ambulance to arrive. My brother told me later that he had walked out the back door of the emergency room and prayed. He had asked his son, Little Rodney—who had died at birth—and his friend, Ross Dutton, who had also passed away after a long, hard battle with cancer. He considers both his angels in heaven. He said he asked them "to go get God and all the other angels together and help Lura."

Moments after those prayers to God and his angels, the ambulance arrived. Inside its belly was the flight crew to take Lura to the airport. The fixed wing air ambulance was waiting at Mathis Field.

The flight team from the fixed wing started the transfer process. They had their own method and routine. They received report from the emergency room doctor and nurses, then they got ready to start loading Lura into the back of the ambulance. First, they ran their algorithm. They are required to run it to make sure the patient still meets requirement for air ambulance. Before they even got to the fourth question, Lura had met the criteria.

During this time the EMTs and paramedics that had brought Lura in earlier had come back in on another run. They were there when the flight crew had finally gotten Lura ready to load into the ambulance to go to the airport.

Prior to putting Lura into the ambulance, the EMTs; paramedics; other doctors who were not even responsible for Lura's care; nurses; everyone in the lobby; Duder; Lora Lea; and Sherri Harris stood to pray for the team and Lura. With tears in his eyes, Duder told me it was an extremely profound moment. Each person placed one hand on Lura and their other hand on the person next to them. They prayed, and Sherri anointed Lura's head with oil.

A second passed when the spell broke, they separated. The rush began again instantly. They loaded Lura inside the ambulance and closed the doors. The ambulance drove off toward the airport and left them to stand and watch her go.

My parents, Lura's father, Chad, and those standing there with them had no idea if this was the last time they would ever see her alive.

The fixed wing air ambulance at Mathis Field, just
after loading Lura, headed for San Antonio.

My parents headed home after the ambulance drove off. Lura's mom, Lora Lea, rode in the ambulance with her. Her father and Chad followed behind in his pickup. My mom called me to let me know Lura was headed to the airport. At that point, I was about an hour and a half out of San Antonio.

*****

I remember laughing and telling my mom, "Well, God is making a way. I haven't seen a police officer since I left the house. Usually by now I would normally see about five."

I had Imili call Lakewood to update the prayer warriors and let them know Lura was in the air. I kept telling myself and my daughter, "Lura will be fine." I kept believing that she would wake up, that she had just been in an extended postictal state. She had experienced repeated seizures, making this a real possibility. But deep inside, hiding in the shadows, fear had let his cousin inside through the back door. Doubt had snuck in while I was busy driving and worrying about my niece. Still almost two years later, I cannot imagine the war that my brother and sister-in-law must have been fighting with these twins—fear and doubt.

My brother had to follow by land because the space on the plane only allowed the pilot, two medical personnel, stretcher with patient, and one other person.

My sister called and said as soon as she was off work she was heading to the hospital. I told her they were bringing her to Methodist Children's Hospital. Then I told her I love her and would see her there. I then kicked in a little faster.

Meanwhile on the other side of the divide, my brother and Chad were headed toward San Antonio via *ground flight*. I laugh every time I think of this because Chad told me later when we were in the waiting room that his faith was diffidently stronger when he got out of Duder's pickup than when he had crawled in it. He laughed and told me he never actually looked at the speedometer but that he had checked a couple of times to make sure the seat belt was working. He said he remembered thinking that God must have had his hand on their pickup because the retaining walls were a blur. He said he

29

remembered thinking if they were off as little as an inch, it would be the end for both of them.

*****

Once we parked in the Methodist Children's parking lot, we headed straight to the emergency room. Imili and I had no idea how long Lura had been there or what was going on. What we found out was that they weren't even there yet. The ambulance was en route from the airport.

Remember earlier when I said you would hear the story of the respiratory therapist? Well, now is that time. But first, let me add this little tidbit. As the fixed wing air ambulance was coming into San Antonio. The air traffic controller told them they had clearance but to bring it in as quickly as possible (they had three jumbo planes in a holding pattern; we are talking *three* international flight jumbo jets in a holding pattern in the third largest airport in the state of Texas) so that Lura's plane could land.

As they were loading Lura into the air ambulance in San Angelo, the flight nurse had them readjust Lura three times. She said she wanted to be able to get to Lura in any place that she was needed. The truth was when they circled the airport in San Antonio and started descending, Lura was still unresponsive and had no way to protect her airway. She was still strapped down in a supine position (flat on her back) for stabilization and safety.

She began to throw up. The respiratory therapist that was at the head of the stretcher was the only one who could get to her and suction her. This prevented her from aspirating—in layman's terms, drowning in her own vomit.

Lora Lea said when they landed and were rolling up the runway tarmac, she could feel the undercurrents from the large international jumbo planes landing behind them. They landed so closely behind them that they were actually rocking their plane as the fixed wing ambulance was rolling up to the ground ambulance.

I was standing outside in the ambulance bay waiting for their arrival. Less than fifteen minutes later, an ambulance backed into the bay. I had no idea if it was Lura's or someone else's.

I remembered I stood stone-still and watched as the ambulance drivers got out and walked to the back of the ambulance and opened the doors. My sister-in-law stepped out of the back of the ambulance. The look of total uncertainty and horror on her face broke my heart. I moved forward on numb feet as they unloaded Lura's gurney. My sweet and beautiful niece looked like she was sleeping and perfectly healthy except for the tell-tale twitching indicating she was still having seizures. She was still unresponsive. I walked behind the gurney as we hurried across the space and into the trauma bay in Methodist Children's where the process begun again.

The ambulance crew and I moved Lura from the gurney to the stretcher. Lora Lea was talking to the nurse and admissions people. Torrie, my sister, had arrived by this time; and we were taking turns staying with Lora Lea and Lura. I was fielding calls from my brother and his copilot Chad. They were coming ground-air on the "Duder Airlines" express trip from San Angelo to San Antonio.

The emergency room doctor arrived, and another slew of tests were ordered—including a second toxicology screen, another lactic acid screen (in case the level had increased since the last one), and most importantly a lumbar puncture (spinal tap in layman's terms).

At this point, they were thinking meningitis. They redrew all the labs before transferring her to a procedure room. During this lull in activity Lora Lea and I talked about the air flight there and how God had aligned everything right down to the air flight crew. The respiratory therapist that had suctioned Lura flew with the fixed wing and not the helicopter, so maybe that was the reason they had to wait for the fixed wing.

Another instance of God lining things up was Duder and Lora Lea's former pastor Glenn who had moved to South Texas just happened to be in San Antonio that day. When he got the news, he headed to the hospital as well. He actually beat all of us there and was waiting in the emergency room's waiting room when we arrived.

I did not know him; so when Lora Lea spoke to him, a huge weight was lifted off of me. He prayed quickly for Lura and Lora Lea and for a safe trip for Duder and Chad. Then he took over the responsibility of Imili in the waiting room.

This allowed me to focus my attention on what was happening with Lura and not having to run out to the waiting room every few minutes to check on her. I knew she would be kept safe.

Hours 6–10

Duder and Chad arrived at this point. I might add at the exact time that they needed to be there, they walked in right before they started their first lumbar puncture. There are no words to describe the look in my brother's eyes.

I knew how helpless he must have felt. He had always been the fix-all for Lura, and at this point he could only stand and wait like the rest of us. All we could tell him was his child was still seizing and unresponsive. All the lab tests had been rerun, and they all still showed nothing conclusive. So now this lumbar puncture was being performed because the emergency room doctor suspected either bacterial or viral meningitis.

The horror in my brother's eyes was replaced with relief for a brief second. Then they returned to stark horror as he listened to the nurse explain the lumbar puncture procedure so that they could understand and sign consent.

My brother and sister-in-law knew what a lumbar puncture is; but when you hear it being explained in the process of giving consent for your child, it changes everything.

I understood that brief flash of relief in Duder's eyes. Fighting a known entity was better than having absolutely no idea what you are up against. Everyone drew in a slow, deep breath when we were placed out in the hallway to wait as the procedure room curtain was drawn.

The whole time, Duder and Lora Lea's phones were blowing up and going off like fireworks. Text after text came in from people who prayed for and are concerned for Lura and for them. I will place just a few of the hundreds of them they received during those thirty-six hours here. Duder or Lora Lea's responses will be in italics.

1. How is Lura?
   Still unresponsive and running more test.

   I am at church and putting her on our prayer list. Also Wanda Holik sends her prayers too.

2. So sorry Lura is not healing as she should. She is in my prayers tonight and each night. I will add her to church prayer list tomorrow. God be with you. You all are like family to us.
3. Hi … thinking and praying. How is it going?
   This is Chad. I am with Duder. They have probably made it to the hospital by now. We should be there in an hour. She is still nonresponsive.

   Be careful when you put the landing gear down. Tell him I am glad you are with him. And we love him.

4. I am out of my doctor's appointment how are things?
   She is still in MRI. Do not know anything yet.

5. This text was sent because during this time Michael's kept calling and disturbing Duder and Lora Lea because they did not want liability for Lura's accident. This return email is from Brad Goodwin:

   I just called and left a message on Scott Riley's voicemail letting him know that you guys asked that I field any and all questions he might have and left him my contact numbers. I doubt that you will have any more contact from him but if you do let me know. You have my cell phone number. Tell me whomever you don't want to deal with during this time and I will take care of it. Whatever Toni and I can do please don't hesitate to ask, and know that we are praying for Lura and all of you!

Brad

6. Hey, boss, this is Shay. I am just checking in on Lura.
7. Shawn Beeles: Praying for Lura and you guys! Asking God to provide wisdom to the doctors. We serve a mighty and powerful God.
8. To Lora Lea's phone: Our prayers continue, and our love is pouring out to you! How is she? Has encephalitis been confirmed?

    She has had a EEG and MRI; however no results for doctor yet

    I think the diagnosis has gone public but not from David or me. Can we tell people?

    Yes, and as soon as we get more we will text.

    At 9:54 p.m.: Are you up?
    Yes.

    How are you all?
    Still unresponsive and seizing despite antibiotics and seizure medicine. Diagnosis confirmed autoimmune encephalitis

9. Hope things are looking up for Lura. The coffee drinkers are praying for Lura, y'all and the treatment. D. Bahlman

10. We are praying and will continue to pray as God heals Lura. —David and Tracy Hettick

11. Praying for you guys. If we can help out in anyway please let us know. —Coach Warren

12. Hey, Duder, this is Mrs. K. Just wanted you to know we are praying for Lura. She is such a sweet kid! I know God is hearing all of our prayers. May God bless you and watch over you guys. We all love Lura and will continue to lift her up in prayer.

13. Just heard about Lura. Just wanted you to know we are praying for her and you and Lora Lea. —Betty Sue

14. Hey, Duder, this is Ivy Pickens. Figured you were still up. Just wanted you to know right now I am praying *big* for Lura. I am praying for fast healing. I am also praying for you and your sweet wife … for strength, comfort. Please try to rest well tonight my friend we are standing in the gap for Lura and your family. Hugs to you all.

15. Hope Lura gets better; the Henry family is praying for her and your family.

16. We are praying for your sweet baby, Duder!

17. Just wanted you to know I am praying for Lura and y'all. I pray God will take her hand and pull her through this difficult time.

18. This is Tonee Ferris. Our prayer team has been praying for Lura all night. God is faithful, and Jesus took stripes on his back for our healing. So stand on the word of God that she is well and whole in the mighty name of Jesus. I continue to stand in faith with your family. I am also praying God to give you all peace that all will be well. Philippians 4:19

19. Duder, this is Amy McCormick … I just wanted you to know how hard I am praying for our sweet Lura and you all. Please be careful traveling. I love that little girl.

The Lumbar puncture was performed. Lura remained unresponsive throughout the procedure. We then began the task of waiting for an ICU bed.

I can remember the clinching of my heart every time I would glance over at my niece—who was always so full of life and high spirits—lying absolutely listless except for the tell-tale twitching of seizures.

The next step was to head upstairs to the ICU. Duder and Lora Lea went with Lura and the nurse who transported her. Glenn, Chad, Torrie, Imili, and I took a different elevator to the pediatric ICU waiting area.

Inside, they were placing the leads for the continuous EEG. The fancy medical term for this is electroencephalography; in layman's terms, though, this is a test that measures the electrical activity in the brain. This was done because brain cells talked to each other through electrical impulses. This was when they placed about forty leads (similar to the ones used to do an EKG of the heart) all over her scalp to monitor her brain activity. Lura was still having continuous seizures at this point.

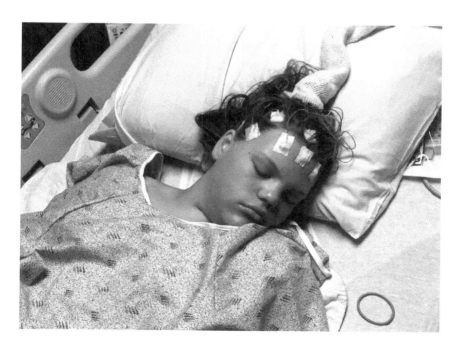

Hours 11–21

*I*t was extremely hard to be approximately fifty feet away from a niece you love beyond words while she lays unresponsive in her ICU bed. Me and all those who love her were sentenced to wait in a small room filled with other waiters.

The lighting was dim during the daytime and even dimmer at night. The temperature in this room hovered just above cold. It was never cold enough to need a sweater or warm enough not to need one.

We sat alone together and hoped, prayed, and believed God would intervene in Lura's case. We tried desperately to send all of our strength and energy to her parents.

All the while, some random television channel ran on and on unnoticed in the background that occasionally caught and held our attention in a distracted way before life grabbed our attention back to reality. We caught ourselves staring at other families huddled together in other areas of the room. Occasionally they'd glance back at us, and their feelings of helplessness were mirrored back as the emotions in our hearts.

In those quiet hours of the night, fear and doubt tried again to take ahold of our hearts. Each of us fought it off in our own way because it felt like a betrayal to Lura and her parents. So each of us fought off fear in tears—the tears we tried to hide from Lura's parents—and made sure we were ready for them when they needed us for anything.

Those duties ranged anywhere from relieving them for a bathroom breaks or just long enough to take a breath of fresh air outside and gather their emotions. The minutes passed as hours, and hours as long, drawn-out eons of time. As I looked back now, I still find it hard to believe that all those hours only totaled thirty-six.

During those hours, I watched the flow of clergy, pastors, preachers, and priests coming to pray for Lura. The ones I can recall were Methodist, Baptist Pentecostal, Lutheran, the archbishop of the Episcopal Church in San Antonio, and the hospital Chaplin. It was truly a sight to see them all join hands and pray for one little girl. Once again, my brother's words echoed in my mind, "That in this wing of the hospital there is no race or class. In this wing, parents wait for the unimaginable to happen." So to see so many different denominations laying down any differences to pray for this child was profound but not surprising.

As each of these people of God passed through our lives, they brought with them renewed strength and faith. They were brief moments of light and warmth against the coldness of fear and the threat of helplessness. Then they would pass from our lives as gently as they had entered it after walking in and asking for the Duderstadt family and left us to return to our vigil, to serve our time as waiters, and to send our silent prayers to God.

During those long, dark hours, Chad and I would talk about life, Duder, Lura and God. Chad and I were as different as the darkness and fear that threatened the stillness of the night in the ICU waiting room and the light and warmth brought by the endless flow of believers that shared their hope, faith, and love with Lura and her parents, as well as the rest of us that loved her and were waiting for her to return from the darkness of unresponsiveness.

We had a chance to really look at what we believed and the reasons behind the rise and fall of my faith and belief. These conversations took us through some of the longest hours of the night.

While we spent our long hours talking, the doctors and nurses continued to flow in and out of Lura's room. They all were saying pretty much the same thing— Lura had autoimmune encephalitis. What this meant was there was an infection somewhere in Lura's body. Instead of fighting the infection, her body attacked her brain.

Dr. Atkinson came in around six in the morning and told Duder and Lora Lea he was going to change the medication. Lura was extremely critical; and if they didn't get ahead of this, somehow Lura would die.

This was a huge blow to Duder and Lora Lea. They sent out urgent texts for more prayers. We posted on Facebook for all friends and family to continue to pray.

I remembered feeling so helpless when I looked into my brother and sister-in-law's faces. I was at my lowest point in my struggle with the twins "fear and doubt."

Suddenly without even knowing what was going to come out, I opened my mouth and the words "my God is not going to let that happen" came flowing out. As my ears heard my words, I realized that I believed them completely.

At least we knew what we were fighting and could shoot an arrow at it instead of the scattered results of a shotgun. So the game plan remained the same—continue the antibiotics, steroids, and seizure medicine, and wait.

Every time we asked, we were told she could wake up in ten minutes, ten hours, ten years, or maybe never. We would look at each other, and we could see the same negation in each other's eyes. Then we would return to the waiting room, and Duder and Lora Lea returned to standing or sitting and staring at Lura as she lay unresponsive in her bed. Inside the waiting room after these doctor's visits, Chad, Glenn, Torrie, Mikel, Imili, and I would go over and over the events hoping to find a weak link in the chain—something we could say, "This. This is what happened."

Then we would pray again. We prayed together and alone. We sat stoically. We laughed. We cried. We tried to sleep. And we drank gallons of coffee as fear hovered in the corner, watching and waiting.

We watched the other families huddle together and go through the same emotions and actions as us. Watching and waiting to see if their unknown would end in tears of joy. If we did not have faith in God, it would seem as if the outcome was just the roll of the dice.

Duder: Hours 1–36

*O*nce again, I will go back to the idea of being a humble servant of God. During my brother's nightmare, he found the faith and courage to minister to other's needs. He had to trust God with the depth to take his eyes off of his child, and attend to the job God laid on his heart.

He and Chad became the official/unofficial prayer warriors for the children and their loved ones in the ICU. They were called upon over and over again by families, nurses, and residents to pray for others.

This happened because of what was happening in Lura's room as she lay there unaware. Believers and nonbelievers alike could not deny the radiant power coming from that room.

At one point, my brother said that he had felt God all day encouraging him to go and pray for this other child and that he had seen people coming all day and night to pray for Lura and no one for their child. He was also aware that the child's family had seen this as well. He forced himself to stand on weak legs and walk away from Lura's bedside. Chad and I were sitting in the waiting room talking when he walked in. He walked over to Chad; and before Duder could say anything, Chad asked, "What took you so long? I have been waiting all day for you to come get me to pray for those kids."

I remembered Duder looking at him for a second then saying, "Okay then, get up. Let's go."

He said he kept watching the faces of the grandmother and other family members of this one child in the room next to Lura's. He watched their faces and eyes as clergies, priests, pastors, preachers, and men and women in the body of Christ kept streaming past their child's room to pray for Lura.

When he and Chad walked in at first, they received one of those quick glances and an eye contact long enough to mark whether or not it was one of their doctors, and then back down. He said that he and Chad continued on in the room, walked up to the bed, and stood there a for second before the grandmother asked sharply, "What are you doing here?"

Duder looked at her and asked, "Do you have anyone to pray for your child?"

She lowered her head and said, "No, we have no one. No one has come in to pray for us."

Duder said, "Well then, we are here to pray for your child."

After that they would go from one room to the next, asking if they would like for them to pray for their child. Some would say yes, others would turn them away. It got to the point when a new patient would come into the ICU the admitting nurse would ask the parents, "Would you like someone to come and pray for your child?"

If they would say yes, the nurse would come and get Duder and Chad. Then twice a day they would make their rounds, praying for the kids. They became part of the fabric that made the ICU while they were there.

Duder told me that at one point he thought, "Is all these happening to my child because I am supposed to be here to pray for someone else's child?"

Or maybe the fact that two strangers in the midst of their own horror and nightmare took the time out to pray for their child, that it might change them in a way that would bring the belief of God into their lives.

God brought Chad into Duder and his family's lives about two years ahead of this event. He worked with Duder at the bus barn in the Wall school district. They were together every day. Chad was the pastor of a small church—the Veribest Baptist Church—and spent his time there as well.

When Lura's illness occurred, they had become friends as close as brothers. So as soon as the call went out Chad came and came, bringing the power of God with him.

Before I go any further, I wanted to say that when I talked to Chad and asked his permission to use his name and tell his part of the story, his first words to me were, "I did nothing but watch the power of God work."

As hard as I tried to explain to him how his faith affected others, his faith allowed others with not quite as much faith to draw a little water from his well. He was just Chad and gave the praise to God. He chuckled, but it was one of those chuckles people used when they were slightly uncomfortable and said, "Sometimes, Duder puts more faith in my faith than I deserve. I am only a man. The praise goes to God."

Chad got to the emergency room and prayed for Lura and then, as I said before, helped Duder get prepared to travel to San Antonio. Duder wanted to make sure when the second the plane left the ground he would be headed to San Antonio.

Chad knew Duder's mind would be distracted, so he helped get clothes, medicine, toothbrushes, and things that could easily be forgotten but necessary. Then he went back to the hospital to pray and wait like the rest of them.

Then he was Duder's copilot on the "Duder Express Airlines" as we jokingly called it. I was sure that if that pickup had wings, it would have taken flight. The point is Chad was there for my brother in those long, terrifying 235 miles. He told me on the way to San Antonio that he and Duder prayed and then he would just let Duder talk. He listened.

*****

Once again, I will mention how different Chad and I are; and here we were left alone together in the long, dark hours of night in the waiting room. Torrie and Mikel had gone home because both of them worked the next morning. Imili was asleep. Duder and Lora Lea were at Lura's bedside. We were all there for the same reason. We were there to send love to Lura.

I will start by asking you if you knew how good pastors and ministers really are. They have that ability to speak to you about everyday events—it is what I called surface talk. Yet they have the ability to bring God into the conversations without bringing out their billy club and bashing you over the head with it.

Well, Chad is one of those guys. I smile now as I write this because I am reminded of his genuine love and faith in God.

To Chad, faith is as ingrained in him as breathing is. I remembered at first, the surface talk from me was along the lines of "I do love and believe in God. I also know he has to exist because I am still alive."

Chad looked at me and started laughing and said, "It is so much more than that. You wait and see."

Then together again we sat in our easy silence and prayed together and alone. We passed those long and dark hours talking like old friends even though we had known each other about an hour before we were exiled to the waiting room together. We hoped, wished, and waited. I was very thankful I learned a long time ago that if I had faith I did not need to beg or bargain with God. I learned the hard way; this is not a sign of extra faith.

Several years ago when I started going to Lakewood Church, I remembered Joel saying something along these lines. He was talking about prayer and faith. This is not an exact quote but close enough to get the point across.

> Praying and believing is not begging and pleading or bargaining with God. The Bible says, "Ask believing and you shall receive. Seek and you shall find. Knock and it shall be opened unto you. For everyone that ask shall receive."

Pastor Joel said in layman's terms,

> If you order something from the store online and pay for it, once the transaction is completed

you don't go back every few minutes and reorder it. You just know it will be delivered.

So when you pray asking and believing, you will receive it from God if it is his will. You have to put as much faith in God as you would an internet store. Don't you think?

This struck me so profoundly at the time. It made everything so clear. So what I was trying to do as I sat in the waiting room was not to let fear and doubt overtake me. I had to keep reminding myself that hundreds of people on six of the seven continents of the world were praying for Lura.

I had also learned over the years that fear and doubt could be false, intimate friends. In my mind's eye, they kept showing me, my brother, and sister-in-law sitting beside their only living child, waiting and wondering whether it would be the lady or the tiger.

So Chad and I did the only thing we knew to do—we waited. While we waited, we watched the flow of people who made the 235-mile one-way trip just to bring love and prayers to Lura and her parents.

They knew Lura was in ICU and that they would only be allowed a few minutes of visiting time. They came anyway.

I watched as person after person asked Chad if he needed a ride back to San Angelo. They knew that he had left everything at a moment's notice. He refused the offers kindly, stating his job was not finished. He was here to pray for Lura and support her parents.

As the hours passed we talked about many different things, but with Chad it always leads back to one thing—God. I remembered at one time telling him that when this is over and done I would have a PhD in God.

For every topic I talked to Chad about, he had a bible verse to compliment his reply. As we all sat and waited, we talked again about the way God had moved the people into Lura's path.

The ICU nurse that took Lura was supposed to be off that night but had switched with someone else. She was extremely good and very caring; this also puts her in line to be Lura's night nurse for three days straight.

The day nurse that Lura had was the cream that rose to the top. I promise you: for one nurse to call another nurse the cream of the crop, you can bet your last cheese cracker he or she is a good nurse.

Going on from there, Dr. Atkinson—the pediatric neurologist that took care of Lura—had the bedside manner of a brick; but sometimes those who are truly so good at what they do usually have so many things and so many children in their minds. It is not an intentional thing. They just come across that way.

He was very good and very competent. He covered every possibility he could cover until we had a definitive diagnosis. That moment, I knew there was more to him than what meets the eye was when I heard him tell my brother, "I have no idea what is happening other than the symptoms she is presenting. I am going to treat every possible cause until we know what is going on." (This statement was made prior to getting the results back from the second lumbar puncture.)

It is a very rare occasion for a physician to admit he has no clue what is happening when statements like that could be misconstrued as incompetence instead of raw honesty. With word of mouth being what it is these days where a statements like that could be placed on social media and be all over the world in seconds, maintaining reputation is imperative.

But Dr. Atkinson had zero qualms saying, "I have no clue. We are going to start over at the beginning and rerun the test. Sometimes a lumbar puncture can give you a false negative."

At this point in the conversation, he asked my brother and sister-in-law for consent to redo the lumbar puncture. My brother's response to him was, "I have already buried one child. My wife and I will not bury another one."

He angrily wiped the hurt-scarred tears from his eyes and met Dr. Atkinson's eyes squarely. I had been watching Dr. Atkinson the whole time. I hope with all my heart that my brother saw and remembered the true raw emotion in Dr. Atkinson's face.

First I saw shock and then compassion. His response to my brother was, "I will do everything in my power to see to it that that will not be the outcome."

I could tell by the look on the nurse's face that was rounding with him that this was not a usual emotion for this man.

The rest of these hours were spent watching as friends and brothers and sisters in Christ continued to flow in and out of the ICU to pray for Lura, one person almost immediately followed by another.

Lora Lea's elderly parents made the trip as well. They came to give their love to Lura and their child and her husband.

At one point, I thought people were astonished to see a hospital clergy, a Pentecostal preacher, a Methodist pastor, and an archbishop of the Episcopal Church all joined hands and in united belief in God, then began to pray for Lura.

I knew at the time I only saw the outside with my peripheral vision. But now looking back on those moments, I remembered seeing other families drawn closer and closer to the circle of faith, and before it was over they were linking hands with us as we prayed not only for our precious child but theirs as well.

*****

Sherri Harris, a Methodist preacher, made the trip as well. She prayed with us and then went and anointed Lura's head with oil.

As I sit here writing about this event, my eyes well with tears at the memory. It was a moment that to me represented God's grace. Even though we believed God would heal Lura, it was that simple act of anointing her with oil that truly relinquished her life into the healing hands of God. The doctors, nurses, and other caregivers may have performed the measures that brought forth healing or death or even years of unresponsiveness, yet it still truly rested in God's hands and only God's hands.

Some of the things that Chad remembered clearly was being allowed to sit with Lura and just be still and humbled by the power of God.

And later when the worst of the worst was over, they were washing the EEG goop and glue out of her hair, and she had wanted Chad with her. He felt so truly humbled, and those pictures he took during those moments he said were treasured memories. He said those moments when he sat with her in ICU after she woke up—all was silent—and her just wanting to hold his hand were true moments of knowing he was standing in the shadow of God.

I will make this statement, and it will sum up not only Chad but also his thoughts on the whole experience. He said, "It was one of the most humbling times of my life: To stand, sit, or be in the presence of God. To know on a core level that every person, believer or not, could feel the power of God radiating out of Lura's room. And to be able to just stand back and watch God work was extremely humbling."

Hours 34–36

*D*uder said he was sitting and praying. He heard a voice as clear as if someone was standing beside him speaking. The voice said, "It's showtime. Stand aside, this show is about to begin."

Duder said, "I told him that he had already put on the most impressive show he had ever seen."

Finally at the thirty-fourth-and-a-half hour, Lora Lea, Imili, Chad, and I had to sleep. We headed to the hotel rooms we had in the hotel across the street from the hospital. We had secured these rooms for showers and catnaps.

We thought, *if we could get just a couple of hours sleep.* We could try and convince Duder he needed to sleep as well by the time we walked to the hotel, showered, and then lay down. It took a minute or two just to unwind even though we were exhausted.

So around the thirty-fifth-and-a-half hour we finally started drifting off. The phone rang thirty minutes later. Lora Lea and I both bolted straight up. Our hearts sank in our chest. We were both coming out of that deep stage of sleep that only the truly exhausted can reach that quickly.

I heard Lora Lea scream and start to cry. My heart took the express elevator to the basement. Then I heard her say, "She's awake!"

The three of us were up out of bed and dressed in less than three minutes. We did not care what we looked like. We just threw on clothes that we could grab. We didn't even brush our teeth.

Duder called Chad as soon as he hung up from Lora Lea, so he met us as we were running up the hotel hallway a little after 4:53 a.m. Then Duder was on the phone to the rest of the family.

What Duder said was he was sitting in the chair, praying. At 4:49 a.m., Lura opened her eyes and spoke to him. He was so deep in prayer that he just answered her without thinking. Then he realized she had spoken to him. He jumped out of his chair. He said he wasn't even sure his feet had touched the floor between his chair and her bed.

He said Lura asked again, "Where's Coco?" That is her little (not-so-little) Chihuahua.

He swallowed his heart back to his chest and told her, "Your dog is at Nanny's."

Then she asked "And can you change the news channel? Why are we watching the news?"

She had no idea where she was or how she had gotten there. She did not believe us at first that she was in San Antonio or that she had come by fixed wing ambulance. Nurses had tears in their eyes as they walked in and out of Lura's room.

She was still very sleepy and was drifting in and out of sleep. Every time she closed her eyes to sleep, our hearts lurched up into our throats. Duder had let Lura talk to Nanny on the phone when she woke up, and my mother had called Becky Callan.

Mom said she told her, "I hate to call you at five in the morning, but our little girl just woke up."

After a long, deep breath Becky whispered, "Thank you God."

Mom said she told her to go back to sleep. She just wanted her to know.

Yes, we had arrived at the mountain top. The Bible says, "Lift up thine eyes unto the hills, from whence cometh thy help." And we were. We were immersed in jubilation and gratefulness.

At about 6:30 a.m., Duder finally left her side and went to the cafeteria in the basement for food. They got their food and coffee and sat down to eat. Suddenly without warning, Duder broke down completely. He wept like a lost child seeing his father's face in the crowd. His tears were tears of relief and gratefulness at what God had just done for them. He said that he told Chad he had seen many miracles in his lifetime, but this is the first time it was a personal miracle.

Chad said doctors, nurses, and cafeteria workers all came over to Duder, asking him if he was all right. Through tears and laughter he said, "I don't know what you believe, but we just witnessed a true miracle of God with my child."

He and Chad both said that they looked so stunned. They were actually coming over to console him. The way he was crying and the fact that they were in a children's hospital, they assumed his child had died.

The fact that his tears were for the complete opposite. They were tears of gratefulness and thankfulness. The doctors and nurses just smiled and said, "Well, we are so glad you got to see that." Then one by one they walked off to their lives at Methodist Children's Hospital.

It felt to me like the rolling of a large stone off of us. So I am sure my next statement will not only sound contradictory in nature but also ungrateful. We were then faced with the reality that she would have to rest. This entailed closing her eyes and going back to sleep. So every time she closed her eyes, we held our breath. Would she go back to the land of seizures and darkness? If she fell asleep, would she wake up again?

The amount of brain damage from the thirty-six hours of continuous seizures had not been determined either. The truth is we told God we did not care how he gave her back to us, just as long as he kept her alive. We would take her; however, he gave her back to us.

This was a true and earnest statement. Yet we had no idea what to expect. She had no memory of anything after going to Michael's. She was still very much worn out from the seizures, and her body ached all over from the fall, the gurneys, and then being in bed the whole time. Her fear and frustration were insurmountable. Those first hours after she regained consciousness were a roller-coaster ride of emotions for both her and us.

We knew that she knew who we were. She knew who she was. And except from not believing us how she had gotten to San Antonio on a fixed wing air ambulance, she knew where she was.

So we returned to our sentence. We waited. We waited to see what would happen. We waited to see if it would be the lady or the tiger. Would she ever have this happen to her again? Would it be tomorrow? Would it happen six months from now? Will she go to sleep and never wake up? We tried to hide our fear from her, because she was scared enough.

When Dr. Atkinson walked in the room after Lura had regained consciousness, he looked at Duder and Lora Lea and said, "This was God. This wasn't me. This was God."

We all cried again.

The next twenty-four hours we spent in ICU were trying not to be caught staring at her when she glanced up at us after a quick nap. The nurse in me stared at the EEG monitor the whole time she slept. Even though she was still on IV antibiotics and seizure medicine, the seizures had stopped. She was able to stay awake longer and longer.

Half way through the next day, Dr. Atkinson came in smiling and said, "We have had no seizures in the last twelve hours. We are going to take off the EEG monitor, and let's see if we can get her a bed on the step-down unit."

The relief that spread throughout us was almost breathtaking. We knew this wasn't over, but this was a giant step in the right direction. This was the time I was talking about when Chad stayed with her as they removed the leads and washed the goop out of her hair.

The Hours and Days
Afterward

Still at the hospital

A couple of hours later, the nurse came in to let us know we had a bed on step-down. Then she glanced at Lura again and smiled. As she turned to leave the room, she wiped the tears from her eyes.

Duder and Chad made their last rounds around the ICU to pray for the kids that would not be leaving the ICU on that day. Eventually, some left in joy, and others died; but as of that moment, they were prayed for by two men who loved God and had just witnessed the bright, shining light of God's hand.

We started the process of packing up and said goodbye to a nightmare. The morning had followed our darkness. We knew we were still walking in the shadows cast by uncertain days ahead. We were not so foolish to believe we were out of the forest, but God had given us a path and light to find our way out.

Dr. Atkinson warned us this could happen again as we switched from IV anti-seizure medications to by mouth, but he was hopeful the worst was over.

The step-down unit was the next step in healing. Now came the eating, the getting out of bed, and walking. Duder and Lora Lea's fear and anxiety ratcheted up. The adrenaline let down hit with both feet. To say their nerves were frayed and rubbed raw by the coarse sandpaper of stress would be an understatement.

In the step down unit

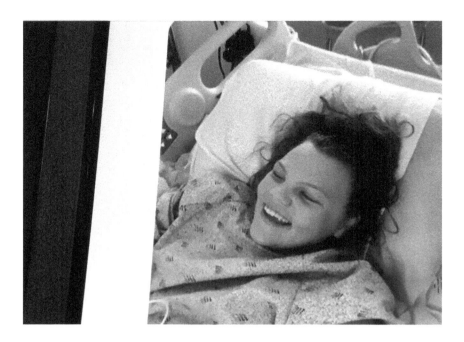

One of my favorite memories in my life was the day I crawled into the shower fully dressed to help her on her first shower after her stay in ICU. At one point, Lura giggled. Now almost two years later, I could hear the sound in the corners of my mind; and I was helpless against the smile that graced my heart and the tears that stung my eyes.

Then the time came on day four that Duder had to go home. There was something at work that he was the only one licensed to do. Chad packed his things, and we all said our goodbyes after one last prayer.

Duder said walking out of the hospital and leaving Lura there was terrifying. He was afraid to take his eyes off of her. But one thing we had all learned—some had come by that knowledge the easy way, and the rest of us had learned it the hard way: life goes on with or without you. So Duder and Chad went home.

*****

I know it doesn't seem like I have talked about Lura's mother a lot. It isn't for any other reason than. She stood watch over her child in a quiet watchfulness. She never left her side.

I know my sister-in-law, and her personality is not the silent-in-the-background type; so I know in my heart how profoundly she was shaken by this event. I have also chosen to close this story with her words. I believe they will speak for themselves. Everything you need to know about my sister-in-law is in her words.

Duder made the 235-mile trip. Chad returned to his family and church. Duder said he did all the things that needed doing at the house. He washed his and Lora Lea's clothes and packed them some clean ones.

He packed a bag for Lura. Now that she was awake, the hospital gown wasn't going to cut it, especially on her walks up the hall. Afterward, he spent his night giving thanks to God for his daughter's life.

The next morning, he went to work. He did his job as effectively and quickly as possible. Then he headed back to San Antonio.

I don't think I have mentioned yet that Lura only eats two foods. She eats chicken *and* chicken. Also, not just any chicken but Chic fillet or Cane's. So while Duder was away, I became the official chicken runner.

What I can say about mine and Lura's relationship is this: we've always had a close relationship. But after we walked through the valley of the shadow of death together, our relationship turned very different. There is a bond there that is stronger than aunt and niece. We also became friends. But when someone takes you to the cliff of life and death with them and came back together, it would change the way you love each other.

I also believed that this time in our lives changed my brother's and my relationship as well. We loved each other, but we loved each other from a distance and in short periods. Now I feel like our relationship is close, and the distance is gone.

*****

On day seven, the discharge process began—setting up appointments and follow-up tests. They had to call the pharmacy in San Angelo to make sure they got enough liquid Keppra (her anti-seizure medicine) as well as liquid steroids and antibiotics. (Remember, I told you in the beginning Lura doesn't do pills.)

They had to line up physical therapy because Lura had a gait disturbance and wasn't walking just right. She needed a cognitive therapist as well. She would be homebound schooled as of the moment, so all of those arrangements had to be done.

Finally on August 8 around noon, Lura went home with her parents. I headed back to Houston.

HOME

*O*nce they got back to San Angelo, another reality set in. They would be at home alone with Lura. They were terrified to take their eyes off of her. They were afraid that she might have another seizure in her sleep or go to sleep and not wake up again.

The long hours of waiting and watching began again. They both took turns, missing work to stay with Lura. Duder, at some point, would take Lura to work with him. They knew she could not be left alone; even if she could, they couldn't.

At night they took turns sleeping with one eye open in a chair next to Lura's bed. Needless to say, the wear and tear on their bodies and nerves increased with each passing hour.

They were all exhausted mentally, emotionally, and physically. Lura was going through her own struggles. She was afraid that if she went to sleep she would die, so she became frazzled as well. Tensions ran high, and exhaustion ran higher. I knew they did whatever they had to do for Lura.

*****

By the end of the second week when it was time to go back to San Antonio for her first follow-up and follow-up EEG, they saw the doctor first and then headed over to have her EEG.

They went in to the place where they were going to have the outpatient EEG. Duder and Lura sat down while Lora Lea went to sign them in. There was an elderly man sitting in the waiting room when he heard Lora Lea say Lura's name.

The man turned and told Duder, "I know about Lura's story. My wife and I and the Crest nuns have been praying for her."

Duder swears to this day he had never seen the man before in his life. He said he remembered telling the man, "Thank you."

Lora Lea came back, and Duder turned to tell her what the man had said. Lora Lea asked, "What man?"

When Duder turned around and was going to point the guy out to Lora Lea, the waiting room was empty except for them.

Duder asked me, "What are the odds of us coming over two hundred miles for a follow-up appointment and meeting someone I had never seen before who not only knew Lura's story but was praying for her as well?"

My thoughts at the time were, *What are the odds of a random dove flying into Belinda's glass door and leaving an imprint on her door so vividly that she took a picture of it and by doing so placing the angel in mom and dad's yard two days before this all happened?*

*****

After their appointment in San Antonio, they headed home. Our grandmother on my mother's side of the family died when we were very young. I think Duder was only about six.

He mowed the graves when they needed it, but really there were not many memories of her for him. So imagine his surprise when they passed by the cemetery that day when he heard her voice—clear as day—ask, "You know we were with you in San Antonio, right?"

He said he just started crying and called mother to tell her what had happened.

It's been almost two years since that Tuesday in August. There has been many ups and downs, numerous hours of medicine, therapy, home school, half days at school, and finally returned to school full time. There has been countless sleepless nights, tears, laughter, moments of praise, and thankfulness.

But when all was said and done, we have a beautiful, healthy, normal teenager on our hands. She never had another seizure. The seizures were one of the symptoms of the autoimmune encephalitis.

This changed all of our lives and affected many others as well. I just wanted to share it with the rest of the world in hopes it would encourage someone in their time of need.

This is a picture of Lura two weeks after
she came home, sitting in church.

This is the prayer blanket that was given to her that day in church. Each person in the church tied a knot in the fringe. As they tied the knot, they said a prayer for Lura. This took place while she was still in the hospital. They left one knot untied for her to tie and say a prayer of thanksgiving when she received it.

The next picture is of Lura and I together.

FREDNA DECARLO

Lora Lea

As promised before, I said I would end this book with the speech Lora Lea gave at church the day Lura received her prayer blanket:

Let us go to the Lord in prayer.

Father, thank you for giving us the faith to believe in Jesus as our savior and for including us in your family. May our life reflect your influence, and I give you permission to make us into the people you want us to be. Please continue to fill us with your Spirit so that we will more closely reflect you in all that we say and do. In the name of Jesus, I pray. Amen.

We are followers of Jesus who is the king of glory. We are full of glory because he is our king. We are brothers and sisters in Christ. We rejoice because God our father and the Holy Spirit live in our hearts. We are full of joy because Jesus wants to give us his peace. Let us share this joy now and in heaven forever. How have we experienced this Joy?

From James 1:2–3, "Consider it pure joy, my brothers and sisters, whenever you face trials of many kinds. You will know that the testing of your faith produces perseverance."

Galatians 3:5, "Does God give you his spirit and work miracles among you because you observe the law, or because you believe what you heard?

This is a story about Lura's miracle and the joy it has brought us. It is not intended to take away from anyone else's great encounters with God's great power.

Tuesday, August 2 of this year was like any other day. Lura and I were shopping in Michael's for craft supplies.

Lura suddenly fell down in a tonic-clonic seizure. The lights were on but nobody was home. 911 had been called, and I called Duder, screaming to get there. Lura was still seizing upon both Duder's and then the EMS's arrival.

EMS quickly got her to the hospital. Duder remembered, as he was following us in the ambulance, saying to God, "How did we get here? Help Lura."

After arriving at the hospital emergency room, Lura was continuing to seize even after all the medicine they had given her to stop the seizures. The problem was she was still seizing.

With the CT scan and blood work all coming back normal, the doctor knew something was majorly wrong but did not know what.

By this time calls had gone out to family, David, and Sherri (both our pastors). Duder had called Chad Leutwyler, a prayer brother in Christ and the former pastor of Veribest Baptist Church. He was in Robert Lee buying a new car. He was at Community Hospital in a little less than twenty minutes.

He had already begun praying for her in the meantime as he drove. David and Sherri arrived at the hospital and many other faith friends started showing up. Text were being sent out and calls were being made. The news spread like a Texas wildfire.

Carmen Dusek received a call from James on her way home from Junction about Lura. She sent out a text regarding Lura's condition to her contacts.

Glenn Luhrs received that text. He called to let them know that he was already in San Antonio.

Lura needed to get to a bigger hospital with specialists that we don't have in San Angelo. An air ambulance out of San Antonio was called.

The team was put of flight time and a new crew had to come in. This delay took hours, but it felt like days when Lura was still unresponsive.

Duder remembered going to the back door and looking up to heaven and asking Little Rodney, our saint with the Lord, to help get us a plane to San Angelo.

Lura was critical with no improvement. He also talked to another member of the great witness above, Ross Dutton, with the same request.

At that second, the ambulance to take Lura to Mathis Field (the airport in San Angelo) arrived. Duder knew that moment that God was in control.

Lura was encircled by EMS, pastors, nurses, doctors, and faith friends and family to pray for Lura's health and safe journey to San Antonio.

Lura was loaded on the plane to head to San Antonio. About Junction I was praying and the Holy Spirit came to me. I felt peace come over me, and I knew that Lura would be okay. Although I did, when or how.

As the plane approached San Antonio, international planes were put into a holding pattern so the ambulance could land. The tower told us to get off the runway as soon as possible.

A Southwest plane landed so close behind us. I could feel the draft when it landed.

It was then off to Methodist Children's Hospital by ground ambulance. When we got to the hospital, Carl Rohlfs, Glenn Luhrs, and my sister-in-law were there waiting and were there to pray for Lura.

Lura was sent directly to the trauma bay. Another CT scan of her head, a lumbar puncture, and more new and repeat blood tests were done.

By this time, Duder and Chad had arrived by ground flight from San Angelo in two hours. Chad said that his faith had increased with Duder's driving.

After all the tests were done, we still had no answers as to what was wrong. Lura was sent to pediatric intensive care. When Lura arrived in the PICU about two in the morning, she began to run fever.

This gave the doctors some ideas that she had some kind of infection going on. They began treating her with what's known as the shotgun approach. She was given strong antibiotics and antiviral medications, as well as anti-seizure medicine.

We stayed by her bedside and did not take our eyes off of her for the next twenty-six hours. During this very trying time, we felt God's loving arms wrapped around us with visits from the likes of a Texas ranger and his wife to pastors, chaplains and archbishops, preachers of many denominations, and even a lone San Angelo fireman.

Each would come into the PICU and pray over Lura. They each noted that she would be on the prayer list at their church. We were bathed in prayer by fellow believing Christians from all over the world.

The Costa Rica mission team to our new friends in France, even though we did not ask for this, we are grateful that God chose Lura and us to show the world of his great healing power, his grace, and his love for all of us to receive.

Jeremiah 29:11 says, "'For I know the plans I have for you,' declares the Lord, 'plans to prosper you and not to harm you, plans to give you hope and a future.'"

One of the most recognizable scriptures in the Christian faith comes to mind at these times. The fourth verse of the 23rd Psalm, "Even though I walk through the valley of the shadow of death, I will fear no evil, for you are with me."

Those were the darkest times of our lives other than when Little Rodney died. We had the steadfast knowledge and trust in the Lord that he would bring Lura through this valley. And she would be better off than when she started.

Lura remained unresponsive for yet another day. Her pediatric neurologist came around six in the evening and told us that Lura was very critical. He was going to change the medication or she was going to die.

This was a huge blow for us. We once again sent out texts to our prayer warriors back home and abroad. One person who received one of these texts put it on their Facebook page, and it was shared. People told us they were up all night praying for Lura. My sister-in-law, Duder's sister

36 HOURS AT THE INTERSECTION OF MERCY AND GRACE

Fredna, said, "My God is not going to let that happen."

About three o'clock that morning, Duder asked Little Rodney to go get every angel he could find, grab Ross and God to get here soon. He said he knew where they were and that they were listening. In Ross's earthly walk with the Lord, he had great faith and conviction.

About four o'clock that Wednesday morning, Duder was standing by Lura's bed. And as clear as if he was standing there, he heard God say, "It's showtime. Stand aside, the show is about to begin."

Duder said he told him that he had already put on the most impressive show he had ever seen. At 4:49 in the morning, Lura opened her eyes and asked, "Where's Coco?"

Coco is her dog that she likes to crawl under the table and pester. Duder said his legs were shaking so hard he could barely stand. He knew he was witnessing a miracle.

We were all overcome with joy. Duder said he told God right then and there that he, her mother, and everyone around the world that had prayed for Lura would give him all glory and praise for his handiwork.

When the doctor made his rounds at six in the morning, he said, "What a miracle from God." That statement reminds me of the passage from Mark's gospel in the twenty-fourth verse in the eleventh chapter. It says, "Therefore I will tell you, whatever you ask for in prayer, believe that you will receive it and it will be yours."

In the days that followed in the hospital, we shared with pastors, chaplains, and others

71

what an awesome God we serve. We witnessed to nurses, doctors, and others that they were seeing a miracle as they came into Lura's room. Many rejoiced with tears in their eyes knowing and seeing what Father God had accomplished.

Not only did God grace Lura with his healing power. Early Thursday morning, God was calling Duder and Chad to the room next door. Duder told Chad God has been calling him to go pray for that child. Chad replied, "I thought you would never ask. He has been calling me over there all day."

They went next door, and there was a little boy there on his third open-heart surgery. They prayed over him. When the mother asked them why they came, they told her that God had sent them. After that, they prayed for him many times over the next few days.

Before leaving the hospital we were officially given the diagnosis of autoimmune encephalitis. On Monday, August 8 at 12:09 in the afternoon, I took a picture of Lura in the pickup and sent it out.

To God be the glory, we headed home to San Angelo. On the way home about, comfort Duder looked over at Lura and said, "I know how Jesus's mother felt when he had been raised from the grave and conquered death. He was alive." We felt the same way that Lura back.

Since we have been home from San Antonio, we have been showered with love through cards, food, and general overall help. Lura is homebound from school and doing physical therapy. But tomorrow, she will go back to school half days.

This is our story about Lura. We hope that you have had the opportunity to see how God is the Mighty Healer and the center of the story.

Without him, Lura might not be here with us today. He is the true healer, and is working to restore Lura back to her former self and even better.

In John 11:4 Jesus says, "Be joyful always, pray continually; and give thanks in all circumstances, for this is God's will for you in Christ Jesus." This sickness will not end in death. No, it is for God's glory, so that God's son may be glorified through it.

All of us here at First Church know that God has performed other miracles for members of this congregation. Todd Sanford came by to pray over Lura in the PICU on the way back to San Angelo from Houston with a new ambulance.

We know that Todd received one of these miracles too. Lee Pipkin was in the Methodist Hospital next door to the Children's hospital in critical condition at the same time as Lura. He also received the grace of a miracle.

Lee and Lura both came back to church on the same Sunday. Lee said, "It is good to see and be seen." Lura was in agreement with that.

It is our sincere hope that here at First Church can overcome any and all petty differences, and disagreements. Because if it were not for our church family and its coming together, Lura's outcome could have been very different.

So if you ever find yourself or a loved one in a trying situation, don't hesitate to call on your church family to pray for you and your family.

Before I close, here is one last scripture Joshua 1:9: "Be strong and courageous. Do not be afraid; do not be discouraged, for the Lord your God will be with you wherever you go."

God has a purpose and a plan for Lura's life. So when you see her in church, just know that you have seen and been part of a true miracle of God.

Megan Hunnicutt is going to bless us with a song that she felt was fitting for this testimony. It is titled "Blessings."

She sang it to Duder last week. When he told me about it, I said how ironic she chose that song because it is the song that was sung at Lura's baptism.

Glory to God!

Lura with her grandparents at the end of that year.
She graduated eighth grade on the A honor roll.

Rodney and Anna with Lura

Gwen and Kenny with Lura at that same graduation

Lura and her parents, Duder and Lora Lea

My final words in this book is a secret message that has meaning to only Lura and I: "Double barrel baby, double barrel, we made it through!"

ABOUT THE AUTHOR

*F*redna DeCarlo was born and grew up in West Texas. She is cofounder of Organic Skin Care Evolution and has worked as a registered nurse for almost thirty years. Her previously published works include *Ten Mile Road, Toenail Trail, Cause and Effect, Significant Other, Thoughts and Afterthoughts,* the "Life of a Blanket in the Medical Center" (*Hektoen International*), and "An Unlikely Friendship" (*San Angelo Standard Times*).

One of her motivations as a writer is to teach young adults history in a fun and exciting way. To ensure higher retention for her other content and audiences, she takes everyday situations and turns them into believable terrors.

Thirty-six Hours at the Intersection of Mercy and Grace: Lura's Story is her first Christian book.

CPSIA information can be obtained
at www.ICGtesting.com
Printed in the USA
LVHW020811031218
599060LV00018B/872/P